WHEN CAN I SAY, "I LOVE YOU"?

WHEN CAN
I SAY
I LOVE YOU?

MAX and VIVIAN RICE

MOODY PRESS
CHICAGO

© 1977 by
THE MOODY BIBLE INSTITUTE
OF CHICAGO
All rights reserved

Library of Congress Cataloging in Publication Data

Rice, Max M.
  When can I say, "I love you"?

  SUMMARY: A discussion of dating, love, and marriage for teenage Christians.
  1. Dating (Social customs) 2. Mate selection—United States.
3. Marriage. 4. Love. [1. Marriage. 2. Love. 3. Christian life]
I. Rice, Vivian B., joint author. II. Title
HQ801.R44   301.41'4   76-54926
ISBN 0-8024-9436-6

17 Printing/LC/Year 90

Contents

Foreword

Love, sex, and marriage—what teenager isn't interested in these three words? And what parents don't look for help in putting these words together for their children in a true picture of love?

As the mother of two teenagers, I am happy to write the foreword for the Rices' book, *When Can I Say "I Love You"?* Helping young people through the experience of discovering the opposite sex can be exciting, beautiful, and sometimes devastating!

I believe that God has given to us human beings both *desire* and a *design* for true fulfillment in love, sex, and marriage. Our generation knows all about the desires, but far too little about the design. God made sex not merely as a toy to play with but as a tool with which to love in the total commitment of marriage.

Parents, teenagers, and youth workers will find that the Rices' book provides two important things. It sets out the eternal, unchanging *principles* of the Word of God which deal with this area. And it gives *practical* applications of these principles.

The book will provide some definite answers for those with very important questions. More than that, it will challenge older and younger people alike to think through their own Christian commitment in love, sex, and marriage, in the light of God's good and true Word.

JEAN GRAHAM FORD
(MRS. LEIGHTON FORD)

Acknowledgements

We express our deepest gratitude to our parents, who, by word and example, taught us the worth of a Christian home; to our teenage daughters, who made helpful suggestions and who have demonstrated that the principles taught in the book do work with modern youth; to the thousands of teenagers whose input during retreats at Look-Up Lodge have been invaluable; to Muriel Larson for her editorial suggestions; and to our fellow staff members at Look-Up for their help in so many ways.

1

Plan Ahead

"They love each other so much!" This remark, made by one of our teenage daughters, was not about a newlywed couple. The lovers, her grandparents, have been married for over fifty years.

After twenty years of marriage, I love my wife more than on our honeymoon. It didn't seem possible then, but it has happened.

Surely, ever increasing love is God's intention. But, unfortunately, this is not what is happening in most cases. Remember all those jokes you have heard about marriage? The jokes about the "old ball and chain," the "henpecked husband," the "neglected wife," and all the rest are too often based on reality.

The startling divorce rate proves the seriousness of the problem. Some authorities believe that up to 95 percent of those who stay together do not really have happy marriages. Let's face it. Too many American marriages are tragic failures. Love's young dreams become middle age's nightmares.

Why do things turn out this way? Doesn't everyone

know that love is just the greatest? Just listen to the poetry, stories, songs, and toothpaste advertisements! How can something esteemed so highly fail so miserably?

Some think that love (generally meaning sex) is more readily found outside of marriage. This is implied in the men's club toast, "To our wives and sweethearts. May they never meet!" Today, many believe that marriage to one person for life is unrealistic. They are trying all kinds of alternatives, but none has proven to be the answer. Can it be that "Love American Style" is not the same thing that God, the original Matchmaker, planned?

You don't have to be numbered among the failure statistics. Many marriages do succeed. Ours does. Yours can. How?

Several steps you might take right now can assure a successful marriage. We will discuss these in detail in the chapters that follow. First, however, we must be certain we are thinking straight on three crucial points: *guidance, perspective,* and *preparation.* These are the keys that will open your understanding of the rest of the book.

GUIDANCE—WHOM CAN I TRUST?

You sincerely want to know what is best for your life in the area of dating and marriage. But there are so many conflicting ideas in circulation today. How can you sift through all the various views and come up with the right answer? You have three choices. You can trust your own instincts. You can listen to others. Or you can trust God. Self, others, or God. Let's look at each of these.

Can I trust myself? Are my own feelings a reliable guide? Check the records. Remember that most married people had all the exciting feelings before marriage. They just knew their love was the real thing. But the records show that many were betrayed by their feelings. Why?

When we trust our feelings, we are putting our faith in the biochemical computer we call a brain. What determines the information a computer gives out? Two things: the program and the input.

We inherited from Adam and Eve a computer that was *programmed* to rebel against authority and to want the forbidden fruit. The *input* of your computer is what psychologists call your environment. Everything you have ever seen, touched, tasted, heard, smelled, and thought rearranges the DNA molecules in your brain. Scientists tell us that everything that has ever gone into your brain is still there. Most of it is in your subconscious, but it still affects what you think and do today.

For example, when you were six weeks old, perhaps your mother went to the grocery store without you. Your computer recorded insecurity, fear, loneliness, and frustration. Then your mother came home. Your computer recorded security, love, belonging, and acceptance.

Seventeen years later you are out on a date and temptation comes. You must decide what to do. Your DNA molecules begin to whirl. Your computer not only remembers the time when you were six weeks old, but also remembers the recent times when you stayed home alone while your friends were going out. Your computer tells you to go ahead and get that warm, secure feeling. Your boyfriend thinks you are yielding because you like him. He doesn't know it is because your mother went to the grocery store when you were six weeks old! Of course, this is greatly oversimplified. But you get the point, don't you?

If I am adding a hundred figures in a computer, how many wrong figures do I have to put in before I come up with the wrong answer? Just one. Even though ninety-nine figures are correct, the one incorrect figure will make me come up with the wrong answer. Do you want to put your faith in that messed up computer you inherited from Adam, with only a fraction of the world's information, and much of that wrong? The Bible says, "A man is a fool to trust himself! But those who use God's wisdom are safe" (Proverbs 28:26, TLB*). We will say more about God's perfect computer later.

OTHERS

What about listening to others? Unfortunately, most people get their ideas of love from songs, movies, television, magazines, and books produced by people who, in many cases, have been notoriously unsuccessful in their own marriages. George and Nena O'Neill's book *Open Marriage* was on national best-seller lists for over forty weeks during 1972 and 1973. In 1974, Dr. and Mrs. O'Neill filed for divorce.

Professional marriage counselors and secular teachers of courses on marriage and family do not have a much better record. At a recent conference on the family, we heard that one organization that trained family counselors was having problems because 81 percent of their counselors' own marriages had broken up.

The Living Bible.

As a young person, you may not be acquainted with any of these would-be authorities. More than likely you are just following the customs and patterns of your peer group. What is their record? Mothers under age twenty are involved in more than 50 percent of all divorces. If both husband and wife are still teenagers when they are married, they do not have even a fifty-fifty chance of staying married five years.

On top of all this evidence from current events, we have the clear teachings of the Bible that the majority of people are on the wrong path. The majority were wrong in Jesus' day (Matthew 7:13-14), and Paul said it would get even worse as we approach the end (2 Timothy 3:13). His statement that people would be "ever learning, and never able to come to the knowledge of the truth" (2 Timothy 3:7) is certainly true of this generation.

Jesus told us that at His return, it will be as it was in the days of Noah (Luke 17:26), when only one family was right, and as it was in the days of Lot (Luke 17:28), at Sodom, when only one man was right. If you were in style in the days of Noah, you were wrong. If you were in the majority, you were wrong. Jesus said that there would be another day like that.

So both the Bible and experience show the foolishness of following the customary styles and patterns of courtship. But if we cannot trust ourselves and we cannot trust others, whose guidance *can* we trust?

GOD

Remember our discussion of our messed up computer and God's perfect computer? Hear what God's Word says:

> Trust in the LORD with all thine heart; and lean not unto

thine own understanding. In all thy ways acknowledge him, and he shall direct thy paths (Proverbs 3:5-6).

I will instruct thee and teach thee in the way which thou shalt go: I will guide thee with mine eye (Psalm 32:8).

For this God is our God for ever and ever: he will be our guide even unto death (Psalm 48:14).

Where do we find the printout from God's computer? It's called the Bible. Remember that a Christian is one who is saved by faith. Part of saving faith is that we put our faith in His computer instead of our own. Isn't that really the smart thing to do? If you think it is, you need to consider our second key idea.

PERSPECTIVE—WHAT IS THE OVERALL PICTURE?

We must see romantic love, courtship, and marriage in the overall context of man's total purpose under God. Jesus makes it plain that if we put any human relationship—mother, father, husband, wife, children, girl friend, boyfriend, or anyone or anything else— above Him, we cannot be His disciples (Luke 14:26, Matthew 10:37). We are to seek the Kingdom of God *first*.

This means that all the decisions of life—marriage, vocation, education, lifestyle—must fit in with our purpose to glorify God in everything we do. It could include the possibility of remaining single.

Would that be a disaster? Not at all. If that is God's choice for you, you could not be happy any other way. Many Christians will testify that they had to reach the point of being willing to stay single before God led them to the one they were to marry. The whole point is that God Himself is to be our *first* love.

Does bringing God into everything take away earthly

14

romance? No. It makes it better. Remember that God is the original matchmaker. Over 300 years ago, Richard Lovelace said, "I could not love thee, dear, so much,/ Loved I not honor more." Substitute *Jesus* for "honor," and the statement is even more meaningful.

PREPARATION—IS IT NECESSARY?

You have chosen God as your source of guidance. You have decided to set romance in its proper perspective. Now does a lovely, gift-wrapped package, labeled "Love—Courtship—Marriage," just fall into your lap one happy day? Sorry! It doesn't work that way! The name of the game is *preparation* according to *God's instructions*.

Marriage is wondrously complex, because two complex, individualistic persons unite to become one flesh. The greater the complexity of anything, the greater the need for adhering strictly to the plans of the designer.

Our Designer has given us detailed instructions for marriage. If we carefully follow them, we will experience the joy and satisfaction we expect, instead of the misery so often experienced in marriage.

Being a successful husband or wife is more difficult than being a successful doctor or lawyer. If you do not believe it, just look at the great numbers who succeed in their professions but fail miserably in their marriages.

Would you submit to surgery performed by a doctor who learned his trade by watching television medical shows, reading doctor stories, listening to drug commercials, and reading a how-to manual just before beginning practice?

Think how much time and money could be saved if

doctors could become qualified this way. Why is a person who wants to be a doctor willing to spend years in premedical training, taking courses which have no direct bearing on healing but which provide a foundation on which to learn? Why is so much of his time in medical school spent learning principles and fundamentals? Why is time spent as an intern, practicing the various required skills? Because no one has discovered a shortcut that produces satisfactory results.

Why should you put forth the effort to develop yourself into the kind of person who can be happily married? Because there is no shortcut. So you will want to avoid future heartaches by taking steps now to prepare for a successful marriage. Since everyone agrees that love is the basic ingredient of a good marriage, your first step in preparation must be to understand what love really is.

Before giving you our specific suggestions, we want you to know that these ideas have been discussed with thousands of teens at our Christian retreat center. Audience response has enabled us to keep what is workable and eliminate the rest.

In addition to teen retreats, we also conduct retreats for couples and families. These retreats have helped us to see what kind of preparation for marriage is needed.

As we examine God's plan in the chapters that follow, some may seem farfetched to you. That should not surprise you. God's Word says, "For my thoughts are not your thoughts, neither are your ways my ways, saith the LORD. For as the heavens are higher than the earth, so are my ways higher than your ways, and my thoughts than your thoughts (Isaiah 55:8-9)." Just remember, God's plan works. The way of the world does not.

2

Understand Real Love

How do you know when you are really in love? "I know it's love," you say. "I have all the classic symptoms. I think about her all the time; I get butter-flies in my stomach; I can't eat; I can't sleep; my heart pounds anytime she's near—of course it's love!"

But the question is, are you in love with the person, or are you in love with love? Would it surprise you to know that most people who think they are in love are not really in love with the person? They are in love with the idea of love.

You can see this almost any day at school. Our girls came home one day telling us about a guy who had asked a girl to go steady with him; she said no. He asked a second girl to go steady with him; she rejected him. A third and a fourth girl both said they were not interested. He asked a fifth girl to go steady with him, and she said yes! And now he is completely and totally in love with that girl. She is everything to him. She is the only girl in all the world. Why? Because they were truly meant only for each other? No. Because he needed a girl friend, and she was available.

We have a strong, inborn need to love and to be loved. This has been proven in hospitals where infants without parents receive the best of medical care. However, if they are not held and fondled, they do not develop properly.

In addition to this natural desire, there is strong social pressure to have a steady. If you do not, people wonder what is wrong. We search for someone to meet this need for belonging. Some, for one reason or another, are unacceptable to us. Others, whom we like, may not like us. But finally we find someone who meets our needs. We meet his needs. We get together and call it "love". All the symptoms follow. We are in love with love.

Don't you see this happening among your friends? Here is a guy who last year was madly in love with a girl. They really had something big between them. She was the one and only girl for him. Now they couldn't care less for each other. Each one loves someone else as much as they used to love each other.

It isn't so bad when you just go with a person for a while and then break it off. The tragedy comes when you marry and then find that you do not love the person anymore. If you think that couldn't happen to you, remember that most people who marry feel the same way. They think that what they have is real love. But the climbing divorce rate proves that many are sadly mistaken.

This is not written to scare you away from love but, rather, to encourage you to seek the real thing. The Hollywood or *Playboy* version of love just does not work out. Biblical love does.

As we search the Scriptures to discover what love really is, some of the precepts may sound silly to you.

True love is so foreign to the modern counterfeit that you may be tempted to reject it as unreal, unless you are convinced that God is wiser than you are.

What, then, is real love? How do you know when you have it? How can you tell if the other person really loves you?

Let's examine the word *love* itself. The Greeks had several words for love. Unfortunately, we try to make do with one. This causes confusion. There are three important types of love, represented by the Greek words *agape, phileo,* and *eros.*

Agape is the word normally used for God's love for man, man's love for God, and man's Christian love for his fellow man. *Phileo* means intimate friendship and indicates that you enjoy the company and fellowship of the other person. These two words are used in the Bible.

The other principle Greek word for love is *eros.* It refers to physical, sexual love, usually set going by the emotions. The word itself is not in the Bible. But this does not mean that the Bible is silent about sexual love. After all, God invented it, didn't He? More about this later.

You may be wondering which of these three kinds of love is necessary for a happy marriage. The answer is easy: all of them. It is like a three-legged stool. If any leg breaks, the stool collapses. Now, let us examine each type.

AGAPE

The first kind of love we will consider is agape. Agape love considers the object of love to be infinitely precious. Agape desires the very best for the one loved.

It is a self-sacrificing love. This must be the foundation upon which the other loves are built. Agape love, in its purest form, is of God. It is part of the fruit which the Holy Spirit produces in those who are God's children (Galatians 5:22).

Agape love is not a matter of the emotions. It is something we should have for all people, though, of course, we should have it to a much greater degree for the one we marry. You may think that this is not what you are interested in. You are interested in romantic love for a particular person. But unless you have agape as a foundation, the other loves will not last.

Think of love as a pyramid. Agape is at the base; phileo is next; and eros is at the top. If we try to turn it upside down, the whole thing topples.

The Egyptian pyramids have stood storms and winds for thousands of years because they had a proper foundation. If they had been built upside down, the slightest breeze would have toppled them.

A marriage will also stand all the storms and stresses of life if it is built on the proper foundation. However, most couples build a relationship with eros as the foundation. Therefore, their marriage cannot endure the storms that are sure to come. They discover too late that phileo and agape cannot be built on the foundation of eros.

While we were working on this chapter, our daughter Carolyn, a college freshman, home for the weekend, came in from a visit with several friends who are high school seniors. She was distressed over the news that one of her high school classmates, who got married last year, is already divorced. She said the couple stayed together only five months.

In explaining the situation to her friends, the girl said, "He simply was not capable of real love." Now she was not talking about eros, or sexual love. That was the big attraction in the first place. And there was certainly a little phileo, or liking, there. They liked to go to basketball games together. They enjoyed listening to records together. So what kind of love was she talking about that was missing? Obviously, the kind that lasts: agape love.

How do you know if you are capable of agape love? How do you know if the one you intend to marry is? How do you develop it? God has given us a wonderful training and testing place. It is called the home, the family you live with now.

If you cannot exhibit agape love in your home before marriage, you will not be able to in marriage. I know you are thinking that your honey is different from the members of your family. Just remember that your parents thought that about each other, and the ones who marry your brothers and sisters will think that about them. The problems are not with the particular people with whom you live. The problems are in living close to anyone.

It is in the selfish interest of the person you are going with to act lovingly toward you now. But when the drudgery and routineness of marriage set in, her basic nature will come through. If she is selfish in her present home, she will be selfish in your new home. The same is true of you. If you cannot exhibit true love at home, you cannot exhibit it in marriage.

In fact, people generally treat their spouses worse than they do other people. All the jokes about married people are not so funny when they come true in your marriage. One of the big tasks of marriage counselors is to get partners to treat each other with the same consideration they do others. Don't think that you and your mate will be the exception.

One of the biggest mistakes people make is to get married because they cannot stand to live at home. Until you can learn to live at home, accepting and loving the other members of your family, you are not ready for marriage.

What is involved in agape love? First Corinthians 13 tells us. Listed below are love's characteristics. Phrases are from *The Living Bible*, with portions from the Phillips translation in parentheses.

Applications of these verses to everyday life are limitless. We can suggest only a few, some dealing with your relationships at home now, some with the person you may be considering for marriage. Some examples use feminine pronouns, others masculine. They all apply to both.

If you will memorize 1 Corinthians 13:4-8 and ask the

Holy Spirit to teach you how to live these verses, you will find hundreds of other examples. You will also be able to tell whether these qualities appear in your friends.

LOVE IS VERY PATIENT

Suppose a boy says to a girl, "I love you so much I can't wait until we are through school. Let's drop out and get married now." This is not agape love. If he really loves her, he will say, "I love you so much that I want the very best for you. I want our children to have educated parents. I wouldn't think of ruining our chances by getting married now."

The Bible gives an example of this kind of love: "And Jacob served seven years for Rachel; and they seemed unto him but a few days, for the love he had to her" (Genesis 29:20).

Are you and your truelove patient with each other? Are you each patient with other members of your families? It may be possible for you to be patient with each other under the rather artificial circumstances of dating. But if you are not patient now at home, you will not be in marriage after the original excitement wears off.

The Bible specifically warns us to "make no friendship with an angry man; and with a furious man thou shalt not go" (Proverbs 22:24). Many broken homes are tragic examples of failure to heed this advice. Do either of you display short tempers at home now?

LOVE IS KIND (LOOKS FOR A WAY OF BEING CONSTRUCTIVE)

Proverbs 31:10-31 is a wonderful portrait of a virtuous woman. One of the characteristics it mentions is that "in her tongue is the law of kindness" (v. 26). True love leads a person to say the kind thing, to perform the thoughtful deed.

In one of the great love stories of the Bible, Boaz was drawn to Ruth because of the way she treated her mother-in-law (Ruth 2:11). When Abraham's servant sought a wife for Isaac, the test he used was that the girl displayed kindness beyond what was called for (Genesis 24:14).

LOVE IS NEVER JEALOUS OR ENVIOUS (IS NOT POSSESSIVE)

Suppose there is a party planned where the guests are coming in couples. You are unable to attend. Would you want the one you love to go with someone else and have a good time or to stay at home and be lonely? Real love puts the happiness of the other first. In talking with teens, this point usually brings more disagreement than any other, until they think about it.

Some are afraid that they might lose their steady if they allow the person to go with someone else. But think for a moment. Suppose the one you love would be happier with someone else? When is the best time for you to find out? Do you want to wait until after you are married? Of course not! The sooner you find out, the better.

If the only way you can hold someone is by not letting that one compare you with others, you do not have a very firm foundation for marriage.

Another reason for going with others is that each of you will mature and develop more broadly if you relate to a number of different people. Real love will lead you to want to become the best possible mate for the person you will marry someday. A wide range of wholesome Christian fellowship will better prepare you for marriage.

24

I am glad my wife and I each dated numbers of others before we got together, because when we did, we knew it was right and have never had the slightest doubt since.

Jealousy not only limits associations with the opposite sex but often keeps teens from meaningful relationships with others of their own sex. Jill used to enjoy fellowship with a group of Christian girls. She is no longer able to be with them, however, because her boyfriend monopolizes all her time. When he is not with her, she wants to be at home in case he calls on the telephone.

Real love would lead a person to say, "Although I want to spend time with you, I also want each of us to spend time with others." Real love, according to the Bible, is not possessive or jealous.

Henry A. Overstreet, psychologist and philosopher, had this to say:

> The love of a person implies, not the possession of that person, but the affirmation of that person. It means granting him, gladly, the full right to his unique humanhood. One does not truly love a person and yet seek to enslave him by law or by bonds of dependence and possessiveness.
>
> Whenever we experience a genuine love, we are moved by this transforming experience toward a capacity for goodwill.[1]

LOVE IS NEVER BOASTFUL OR PROUD
(ANXIOUS TO IMPRESS)

Have you ever seen anyone display her sweetheart like a trophy? By her actions, she seems to be saying: "Look what I caught. He's mine. I got him." She is anxious to impress people with how much she and her catch love each other.

Our daughter came in one day quite tickled over an incident that illustrates this point. In order to jump on the trampoline at our camp, it is necessary to have four spotters. There were five people there, which should have been ideal: one to jump and four to spot. However, no one could jump because two were seemingly glued to each other and had to be considered as one. What they called love would not let either one move four or five feet away from the other so that all could enjoy the trampoline. Doubtless they thought they were impressing people that their love was the real thing. Not so, says the Bible. Real love is not anxious to impress others.

LOVE IS NEVER HAUGHTY OR SELFISH (NOR DOES IT CHERISH INFLATED IDEAS OF ITS OWN IMPORTANCE)

Since we are in love, members of our family, our friends, and all others should make whatever adjustments are necessary in order that our love should have central place. Right? *Wrong!*

LOVE IS NOT RUDE (HAS GOOD MANNERS)

The basis of manners is thoughtfulness for other people. Lack of good manners indicates self-centeredness. A person who does not show respect and consideration for others now will not have respect for his mate after marriage.

LOVE DOES NOT DEMAND ITS OWN WAY
(DOES NOT PURSUE SELFISH ADVANTAGE)

Often a person saying "I love you" really means "I love me and want you." For example, suppose a boy says, "I love you." Then by his actions, he says, "Because I love you, I'm going to ruin your character, your reputation, your chance for a happy marriage, your self-respect, and your relationship with God. And I'm going to do all this because I love you so much." Does he really love you? Do you want to build a home on that kind of foundation?

If anyone really loves you, he will try to make you a finer, sweeter person. When anyone tries to push you down instead of lift you up, you can be sure he loves himself and is using you.

This does not mean that we are to neglect ourselves or that we cannot enjoy the other person. It does mean that we do not hurt others to gratify our own desires.

LOVE IS NOT IRRITABLE OR TOUCHY

Do you or your true love overreact to instructions from your parents? Do you resent the way others act? Are you easily upset? If so, you are not yet capable of the kind of love which leads to a happy marriage. Work on this at home.

LOVE DOES NOT HOLD GRUDGES AND WILL HARDLY EVEN NOTICE WHEN OTHERS DO IT WRONG (DOES NOT KEEP ACCOUNT OF EVIL)

If the person you go with is very critical of other people, you can be sure he will be critical of you. Maybe not now. Maybe not to your face. But all the jokes about nagging will cease to be funny if you marry a critical person.

LOVE IS NEVER GLAD ABOUT INJUSTICE (OR GLOAT OVER THE WICKEDNESS OF OTHER PEOPLE)

Many people, for one reason or another, refrain from

certain bad things themselves. However, they seem to enjoy thinking about these things and talking about those who do them. Others rejoice in naughty acts and think there is something cute or clever about mischief. The Bible says, "It is as sport to a fool to do mischief" (Proverbs 10:23).

One reason some people gloat over the wickedness of others is that it gives them such excuses as, "Everybody is doing it," "Other people do things just as bad," "It's just the style."

LOVE REJOICES WHENEVER TRUTH WINS OUT

Paul said, "Finally, brethren, whatsoever things are true, whatsoever things are honest, whatsoever things are just, whatsoever things are pure, whatsoever things are lovely, whatsoever things are of good report; if there be any virtue, and if there be any praise, think on these things" (Philippians 4:8).

How do the two of you check out on this? You can tell by what you enjoy reading, watching, listening to, and talking about.

IF YOU LOVE SOMEONE YOU WILL BE LOYAL TO HIM NO MATTER WHAT THE COST (NO LIMIT TO ITS ENDURANCE)

The Bible says, "With all lowliness and meekness, with longsuffering, forbearing one another in love" (Ephesians 4:2). Here again, the home is the ideal training and testing ground.

YOU WILL ALWAYS BELIEVE IN HIM (NO END TO ITS TRUST)

In 2 Peter 1:5-7, we are told that faith is the foundation on which all other virtues are built. Love, the greatest virtue, is the last one added. Anyone who does not believe the truths of God will be incapable of true love. This works both ways. Many young people do not believe God's truth because through lack of love, they are rebelling against their family. In order to justify their behavior, they doubt the Bible.

YOU WILL ALWAYS EXPECT THE BEST OF HIM (NO FADING OF ITS HOPE)

In light of the startling statistics about the high rate of unhappy marriages, most people have very little hope of happiness. Those who trust God, however, have tremendous hope, which will be evidenced by their following the scriptural pattern. "For whatsoever things were written aforetime were written for our learning, that we through patience and comfort of the scriptures might have hope" (Romans 15:4). "And every man that hath this hope in him purifieth himself, even as he is pure" (1 John 3:3).

(LOVE CAN OUTLAST ANYTHING)

In marriage, you will be called on to endure inconveniences, hardships, and misunderstandings. Do you have the love that endures?

LOVE GOES ON FOREVER (NEVER FAILS)

The love we have been talking about never fails. The Hollywood or *Playboy* version often fails before the honeymoon is over. Which do you want?

You are probably pretty discouraged by now. You were interested in romance, and we have taken all this time without getting there. Many people have experienced the same thing in watching a new home being built. They were anxious to see the house go up, and instead the workmen dug down. Builders know the importance of a firm foundation.

Any good football team spends most of its time on

29

fundamentals. Those who master the fundamentals are the ones who experience the thrills later on.

We are now ready to turn our attention to the next kind of love.

PHILEO

Christians should develop agape love for all people. We do not have phileo love for all, however. We have phileo love for a much smaller group, some of our own sex and some of the opposite sex. This is the group that we enjoy being with. Phileo is closer to our word "like".

The pyramid illustrates how the objects of our affection begin to narrow as we get to phileo. As we think of narrowing further to the one we will share eros with, it is extremely important that we are certain that we have phileo love for this person *first*.

Do you enjoy doing things together—other than making out? Do you enjoy working together, talking about important things together, discussing spiritual things together, and playing together? Do you have some common interests?

If you enjoy only physical intimacy, you have a very poor foundation for marriage. It is much more likely that you are in love with love than with each other.

This is one reason it is so important to have a wide variety of meaningful relationships with people of both sexes. If we single out one too soon, we fail to develop the capacity for a strong phileo relationship.

Some may want to work on phileo and eros at the same time. "Why not spend part of the time making out," they reason, "and part of the time talking and doing other things to develop phileo love?" It won't work. To understand why, we must examine the nature of eros.

EROS

Since *eros* is not used in the Bible, we turn to the Greek writers to learn its meaning. The following list contains some typical quotations, from several Greek authors, describing eros: "passionate love which desires the other for itself"; "sensual"; "intoxication"; "sets all the senses in a frenzy"; "no choice is left, nor will"; "ecstasy"; "sensual intoxication and the supreme form of ecstasy."

For Plato, eros was "an ecstasy which transports man beyond rationality."

The modern way of saying much of the above is simply, "Love is blind." If you retain your common sense, you do not have a real case of eros. Remember, this is the opinion of the romantic writers, not that of some stuffy old theologian.

The conclusion should be obvious. If we become blind as soon as eros sets in, we must be sure that we have agape and phileo love first. The answer to the question, How can I know if it is really love? is simply that you cannot if eros develops before you are certain about the other types of love.

Under the influence of eros, you will think that you have phileo and agape for each other. This is one reason for postponing physical intimacy.

To illustrate, suppose you are planning to go out one night. The power company calls and informs you that the lights will be turned off in fifteen minutes. You need to choose socks to match your clothes. Would you

31

want to make your choice before or after the lights go out?

Likewise, if you want to be sure you have agape and phileo love for a person, when do you need to decide? Before the lights go out. As soon as eros sets in, the lights go out. You become blind.

Surely you have seen this in others. You have wondered why one of your friends likes a particular person. What could he possibly see in her? Actually, he is unable to see anything in her. He is blind. Everybody knows it except him. Think for a moment, and you will probably recall many incidents like this.

How do you keep it from happening to you? Postpone physical relations that would result in eros until after the other relationships are thoroughly developed. This, of course, takes time.

Youth often ask about kissing on an early date. If we realize that eros may very well set in with the first kiss, the answer should be obvious. If this seems far fetched, we remind you again to look at the high percentage of unhappy marriages. Do you want to join them?

Remember, most of them "just knew" theirs was the real thing. They never thought they would be blind. Too late they found out they were really in love with love, meaning physical attraction. But doesn't eros play an important part in marriage? Yes, of course, it does. So let's talk in the next chapter about putting sex in its proper place.

3

Sex is Beautiful

Sex is a wonderful gift of a loving God. It is part of His creation, which He called "good." Everyone knows that sex makes possible the continuation of the human race. But God did not limit it to that; He piled on the extras. He meant for it to be the glue that makes marriage hold together, providing for strong, happy homes. And he added to it the bonus of inexpressible pleasure that gives real zest to life.

Do you believe all that? Or have you fallen for some of the distorted views of sex that cause so much unhappiness? One of these is that sex is bad, except when used for reproduction. Another warped idea, opposite to this, is that sex is great, a physical thrill to be experienced whenever and with however many partners you choose; it is just a bundle of purely animal pleasure, with no concern for persons, no commitment or responsibilities messing things up. Let's see if we can disprove both of these mistaken beliefs.

First, with humans, is sex only for reproduction? Try to think logically about this. Be practical. If God had made us male and female only for bringing more males and females into the world, He could have arranged a method like most fish have. The female fish just deposit eggs somewhere, and the males swim along later and fertilize them. It gets the job done, but there is no big thing going between a mama and a papa fish.

Or He could have made us like dogs. They are really more efficient at reproduction than humans. A female dog is in heat only at certain times. If you want her to have puppies, you put her with a male. If you do not want puppies, you isolate her until the time is up. The rest of the time, no sweat, no bother. But this is not the only purpose of sex for human beings.

God wanted us to enjoy life, not just to exist. He proved this by giving humans capacities He did not give animals. For example, most animals are color-blind. Even so, they can get around without bumping into objects. But God wanted man to do more than just get around. So He made us able to see in color.

God could have made everything sound alike, but He wanted us to enjoy what we hear. So He made us able to appreciate fine differences in pitch, tone, and volume. God could have made everything taste alike, but He wanted us to enjoy what we eat. Similarly, He could have made sex a simple means of reproduction, but for humans, He wanted sex to be a great deal more.

The second chapter of Genesis tells us how it all came about. Here we find Adam actively involved both with God and with animals. Then the Bible says, "But for Adam there was not found a helper suitable for him" (Genesis 2:20, NASB*). It was God Himself who recog-

*New American Standard Bible.

34

nized that in all of creation there was nothing that could completely meet Adam's needs.

Our loving God decided to make a new creature for Adam. This creature was going to be enough like Adam so that there could be real fellowship. But this new creature was not going to be exactly like Adam. There were going to be marvelous complementary differences, and these differences would add a wonderful quality to life.

So God put Adam to sleep, performed the operation resulting in woman, and presented this new creature to Adam. What was his reaction? According to *The Living Bible*, the first three words he uttered were, "This is it!" (Genesis 2:23).

Now, the dog is said to be man's best friend, but dogs weren't *it*. Chimpanzees are cute, but they weren't *it*. Elephants can do a lot of work, but they weren't *it*. But Adam looked at this new creature and said, "This is *it*!" Another paraphrase might be simply, "Wow!"

God took the new creatures and established the home. He ordained that a man and his wife should live together as one flesh (Genesis 2:24). He made the family the basic unit of society.

God knew that stable homes would provide the only hope for a happy society. He also knew that there would be terrific problems inherent in people trying to live together in the same home. These problems bring us to another reason God made sex as He did in humans. He created the sex drive in such a way that it could be a powerful force in strengthening the family and making home the happy place He meant it to be.

To understand the need for help in the home, consider where it is hardest for you to act like a Christian.

Where are you most likely to get upset, to be resentful, to be selfish? At home? Who irritates you the most? Most young people say their brothers, sisters, and parents.

Why? Because you have an unusually difficult family? No. Some girl, someday, is going to think that spending eternity in your brother's arms would be fabulous. And some boy is going to get butterflies in his stomach at the mere mention of your sister's name.

Remember that your dad really flipped for your mother, and your mother thought that being close to your dad was just the greatest. The problem is not your brother, your sister, or your parents. The problem is that any time two people live close together, there are frustrations. What is good for one often is bad for the other. If you have one telephone and two people, you have problems.

The frustrations of living with a brother, a sister, or parents are nothing compared to the frustrations of marriage. One partner thinks the child should be allowed to go to a party; the other thinks not. Does he get a new set of golf clubs, or does she get a new coat? Conflicts.

But God meant for us to live in families, so He gave us a powerful psychological, emotional, physical drive: the sex drive. It is a fabulous means of communicating to someone you love, "In spite of the fact that I've been selfish and I've been thinking of myself instead of you, I do love you in a unique and special way. You hold a place in my heart that no person has ever held before, and all that there is of me I commit to all that there is of you, forever." It is a coming together so wonderful that the Bible says the two become one flesh (Genesis 2:24).

We also have other physical ways of expressing love.

36

I hope I love every person on earth, but I don't love everyone the way I love my wife. I love her in a way that is different. In addition to saying it with words, I like to express my special feelings for her with a hug and a kiss.

The physical expression of love is so wonderful that Satan would like to ruin it. Suppose my wife knew that in my case (remember, she used to date me before she married me), physical expression of love did not mean anything special. It was just something I did on a date. The name of the game was how far, how soon. Instead of love, it was exploitation. I would have ruined the opportunity to express in a physical way, the unique relationship we have.

Satan hates happy homes. Since sex, used properly, invigorates marriages, Satan must get us to use it improperly. He has been tremendously successful.

The proper use of sex is described in Proverbs 5:18-19 (NASB) as follows:

> Let your fountain be blessed,
> And rejoice in the wife of your youth.
> As a loving hind and a graceful doe,
> Let her breasts satisfy you at all times;
> Be exhilarated always with her love.

Obviously, God is in favor of romance in marriage. If you are married for fifty years, God wants you to have fifty love-filled years, in which you are exhilarated with the love of your mate.

Assume that you will remain married for sixty years. Your time line would look like this:

DATING	M	A	R	R	I	E	D
5	10	20	30	40	50	60	65

In order that you might rejoice with the wife of your youth as long as you live, God follows the verses quoted above with a warning against embracing someone to whom you are not married.

> For why should you, my son, be exhilarated with an adulteress,
> And embrace the bosom of a foreigner (v. 20, NASB)?

Proverbs 5:3-5 (NASB) also warns us against improper use of sex:

> For the lips of an adulteress drip honey,
> And smoother than oil is her speech;
> But in the end she is bitter as wormwood,
> Sharp as a two-edged sword.
> Her feet go down to death,
> Her steps lay hold of Sheol.

At the beginning of the chapter, we presented sex without responsibility as a second warped view. If we misuse sex, we have surrendered one of the great aids to a happy and enduring marriage.

Two wrong views of sex, then, are (1) sex is bad and (2) sex is something to be exploited.

We have also seen two very good purposes for sex: (1) to increase happiness and (2) to strengthen marriages.

THE SEX DRIVE

In order to put sex in its place, we need to understand how the sex drive works.

God made the sex drive powerful in order to fulfill an important role. Anything powerful can be used for great good or for great evil. Atomic energy is powerful; it can supply our needs for generations or destroy us in a few minutes. The sex drive is also powerful for good or evil.

Compare sex with nitroglycerin. Nitroglycerin is tremendously powerful and therefore can do much good. Suppose that, because it is such great stuff, I decided to toss you a jugful. "Here, catch," I say casually. No! We realize that because it is powerful, it must be treated with care!

There are three ways God could have designed the sex drive. First, He could have made the sex drive seasonal, as in dogs. This would not have done the job. Second, He could have made it constant; but life would have been unbearable. So God thought of a more wonderful way. He designed humans with a constantly potential desire which can be activated by stimulation. Two people stimulate each other to bring about this powerful force which enables them to become one flesh.

Although all the senses are involved in sexual stimulation, fellows seem most easily aroused by what they see and by physical caressing. Since girls are not ordinarily aroused visually, some apparently do not realize that guys are. But some girls know it! They know just how to walk, dress, sit, and move so as to stimulate fellows. A lot of "good" girls either do not know, or else they are not good girls. If they knew, they would not dress and act the way they do. The Bible teaches that if we cause a person with a weak conscience to sin, we have sinned against Christ (1 Corinthians 8:12).

Some use the excuse, "It's just the style." Remember, Christians are told, "Don't copy the behavior and customs of this world" (Romans 12:2, TLB). As we said in the first chapter, we can expect the styles to be wrong: they were in the days of Noah.

Other girls excuse their actions by saying, "If they didn't have evil minds, they wouldn't get those thoughts. What I do has nothing to do with it." Ask a boy if what you do has anything to do with it. If he is honest, he will tell you that it very well does.

Suppose we lit the fuse of a stick of dynamite, and it exploded and demolished the building. Would you say it was bad dynamite because it blew up? Of course not. It was made to blow up. The entire manufacturing process was planned so that when the spark hit the right place, a tremendous amount of energy would be released. It is not bad for doing what it was created to do.

Now if I dropped a match on a loaf of bread and it blew up, you would say that was bad bread. It should not have done that. The question of goodness and badness depends on the purpose. What was it created to do?

Our loving God created men so that physical caressing and certain sights will bring into being a powerful force. We are not to be surprised, therefore, when that happens.

If we don't blame the dynamite for the damage it did, whom do we blame? The person that lit the fuse. Girls, did you ever light anyone's fuse?

Does this let the boys off the hook? Can a boy tell a girl that God gave him those desires, and therefore she must give in? That is not what the Bible says.

Proverbs 6:23-28 (NASB) warns against the dangers of stimulation of the sex drive outside marriage.

> For the commandment is a lamp, and the teaching is
>   light;
> And reproofs for discipline are the way of life,
> To keep you from the evil woman,
> From the smooth tongue of the adulteress.

Do not desire her beauty in your heart,
Nor let her catch you with her eyelids.
For on account of a harlot one is reduced to a loaf of
   bread,
And an adulteress hunts for the precious life.
Can a man take fire in his bosom,
And his clothes not be burned?
Or can a man walk on hot coals,
And his feet not be scorched?

Just as you cannot walk through fire and not be burned, you cannot continually submit to sexual stimulation and not expect to sin.

Suppose you exclaim, "The building is on fire!"

I answer, "It's just natural for fires to burn." Then I pour gasoline on the fire.

You cry, "It's burning worse!"

"I can't help it," I say, "It's just the nature of fires to burn." Then I put more gas on the fire.

Would you think I was stupid?

Suppose a boy has a date for tonight. Before going, he reads a magazine that was designed to stimulate lust. He listens to a tape that is successful because both the words and the beat produce lust. He picks up his girl, and guess how they decide which movie to attend? They choose on the basis of advertisements that indicate which show will create more lust.

After the movie they park in an appropriate environment and he begins an operation specifically designed to produce lust. He then says, "It's just natural. You have to give in."

The Bible says if you walk on fire, your feet will get burned.

We can summarize with this illustration. A boiler with no way for steam to get out will explode. If you are

41

smart, you will not build a fire in one until you know that there is a safe outlet for the tremendous pressure that will be built up. This, quite simply, is what the Bible teaches about sex. It is a wonderful gift of God. But don't build the fire until there is a safe outlet for the tremendous emotional and physical pressures that are built up. The only safe outlet recognized in the Word of God is in the permanence and commitment of marriage.

A WORD FROM JESUS

Let's look now at the teachings of Jesus in the Sermon on the Mount.

> Ye have heard that it was said by them of old time, Thou shalt not commit adultery: But I say unto you, That whosoever looketh on a woman to lust after her hath committed adultery with her already in his heart. And if thy right eye offend thee, pluck it out, and cast it from thee: for it is profitable for thee that one of thy members should perish, and not that thy whole body should be cast into hell. And if thy right hand offend thee, cut it off, and cast it from thee: for it is profitable for thee that one of thy members should perish, and not that thy whole body should be cast into hell (Matthew 5:27-30).

Remember, we said men are stimulated by sight and touch. If you cannot help getting lustful when you look at girls, what do you do? Jesus said to pluck out your eye. If your hand cannot help but wander on a date, what did Jesus say to do? Cut it off.

Is this the voice of a mean old man that just doesn't want you to have any fun? No, this is the voice of Jesus, who came that you might have life, and have it more abundantly (John 10:10). Remember that Jesus takes enough personal interest in us to keep up with every hair on every head (Matthew 10:30).

From His vantage point in heaven, Jesus has seen this force, which was created to bring happiness and to stabilize marriages, used instead to bring untold misery and to break up homes.

He has seen even such great men of God as David overcome by lust. The Bible calls David a man after God's own heart (Acts 13:22). We cannot read the psalms he wrote without being impressed with his spirituality. But David was not strong enough to withstand lust. He was defeated when he saw a woman taking a bath.

Now it was not that first look that got him. Sometimes you cannot help that first look. But David looked again and again. As a result, he shattered the Ten Commandments. Being a true man of God, David later sincerely repented. Psalms 32 and 51 tell us of his genuine remorse. David was forgiven and is in heaven today. However, forgiveness of sin does not remove the results of sin. For example, if I were to kill someone and then later repent and ask for forgiveness, God would forgive me. But this would not bring the person back to life.

David was forgiven, but the results of his sin made his homelife miserable. One of his sons raped one of his daughters. Then that son was killed by still another son, Absalom, who also led a rebellion against David. David, who should have had a good old age, had a terrible homelife because he could not handle lust.

You may think you are smarter than David, but are you smarter than Solomon? The Bible calls him the wisest of men, but he was not wise enough to handle women. He, who had a great beginning, also had a terrible old age. The Bible tells why. Women turned his heart from God.

We can imagine how grieved Jesus is to see these and other great saints ruined because of lust. No wonder He pleads with us with all His love to eliminate anything which creates sinful desires.

A young man at one of our retreats once asked me if it was all right to pet if you knew you were a strong enough Christian to stop before you went too far. I asked him if he was a better man of God than David. Are you better than David? Are you smarter than Solomon?

What Jesus was saying in the Sermon on the Mount is that if there is anything in our life as good, as useful, as unquestionably beneficial as a hand or eye, but it causes us to have lust, we should get rid of it, and get rid of it quick.

If this seems harsh, you may prefer Job's remedy. He said, "I made a covenant with my eyes not to look with lust upon a girl" (Job 31:1, TLB).

Jesus was aware of the law of diminishing returns. This simply means that when you do something over and over, you do not get the thrill you got the first time. For example, the first time a guy holds a girl's hand because she's special to him, it gives him a thrill. It continues to be nice the second and third times. But there comes a time when all he gets is sweaty hands. Then, to get the same thrill he got the first time he held her hand, he puts his arm around her. What a thrill— the first time. This is great for awhile, but one evening his arm goes to sleep on him. The thrill is gone. To get a thrill now, he gives her a goodnight peck on the cheek. Wow! He doesn't walk home: he floats home. He doesn't remember opening the door: he's just home. But this, too, gets old. The same thing happens at each stage. To get the same thrill, there is constant pressure to go further and further. All too many go all the way, thus committing one of the sins about which it is said "that they which do such things shall not inherit the kingdom of God" (Galatians 5:19-21).

Suppose that by the time you have finished high school, you have done everything decent to do on a date. What are you going to do your freshman year in college? And your sophomore year? Your junior year? Your senior year? You see how your chances of remaining pure diminish? This is one reason so many get bored and drop out of school to get married. There is nothing left to do.

A similar point to keep in mind is that once we reach a point of physical intimacy, that becomes our beginning point on the next date. For example, suppose that you have dated a girl a number of times. One evening, after three hours of being together, you finally work up to a kiss. On the next date, it doesn't take you three hours. You begin with a kiss. Then where do you go from there?

Where do you draw the line? Scientists discovered that if they put a frog in a bucket of hot water, it would jump out immediately. But if they put the frog in a bucket of cool water and heated the water slowly, they could cook the frog. He could never decide at what precise point the water became too hot.

Most Christians, if asked if they intend to keep themselves pure for the one they would later marry, would say yes. However, like the frog, many are never able to decide at what point to quit petting. Jesus told us to stop somewhere before lust sets in.

This is one reason for not going steady in high school. The longer you go with one person, the more likely you are to get deeply involved.

A WORD FROM PAUL

Paul also warns of the dangers of sex outside of marriage. In 1 Corinthians 6:9, he begins a list of people who will not inherit the Kingdom of God. The list includes fornicators, adulterers, homosexuals, and drunkards. He repeats, in verse 10, that none of these will have any share in the Kingdom of God.

Often a boy will ask a girl to prove her love by committing fornication. She should tell him to prove his. Obviously, if he really loves her, he will not want her to commit such a terrible sin.

Does this mean that sexual sin is unpardonable? Of course not. After stating, in verse 10, that those who commit such sins would not inherit the Kingdom of God, Paul informs the Corinthians, in verse 11, that they were like that once, but that they have been cleansed through Jesus Christ.

Regardless of how deep we have sunk, if we repent, we can receive Jesus, by faith, as Saviour and Lord and begin again. Can we keep on committing these sins with the idea of being forgiven the next day? No! To continue to willfully practice a life of sin would indicate that we had never truly repented and been saved to start with (1 John 2:4; 3:8).

In 1 Corinthians 6:15-20, Paul continues to teach that our bodies belong to Christ and that members of Christ's body should not be involved in any form of sexual immorality. We are, therefore, urged to flee from all sexual sin.

46

Does this mean that we should have nothing to do with the opposite sex? Oh, no! I am much more concerned about a teenager who is not interested in the opposite sex than I am about one who is. God wants you to enjoy the opposite sex. You cannot mature properly unless you relate to those of the opposite sex as well as to your own.

In chapter 4, you will find ways to relate to the opposite sex that are fun and that are excellent preparation for marriage, but that do not have the dangers usually associated with dating.

What we are looking forward to is that day when you commit yourself to another person for life. As you drive off together, you realize that now the two of you are a family. You stop at a motel and prepare to give yourselves to each other.

You remember that the Bible teaches "Marriage is honourable in all, and the bed undefiled: but whoremongers and adulterers God will judge" (Hebrews 13:4).

If you have trusted God in your dating, you will be so glad you did. You will realize that virginity is a gift that can be given only one time. It can be given only to one person. You will be so thankful you saved this night and this gift for the one you are committed to be with the rest of your life. You will rejoice that you did not give this special occasion to someone who was here today and married to someone else tomorrow.

The two of you will get into bed and have a wonderful time. There will be a complete and total self-giving. There will not be the slightest guilt, holding back, or uneasy conscience which wrecks so many relationships. You will have complete freedom, because you did it God's way.

As you two become one flesh, God is smiling. This is what He had in mind when "male and female created He them" (Genesis 1:27).

4

Becoming Marriageable

You no doubt look forward to someday having a good, lasting marriage. But in order to do so, you yourself have to be a good marriage risk! How do you become this? Work on the fundamentals!

One day I was watching a football game on television. In the last two minutes of the game, a halfback broke loose, crossed the goal line for the winning touchdown, threw the ball straight up in the air, cut a somersault, and jumped up and down shouting. To me that was the most thrilling part of the game! Every player would like to experience a thrill like that.

So, what do you expect to find everybody doing at football practice? Do they practice running across the goal line and throwing the football up in the air and jumping and shouting? That's the thrilling and exciting part, but is that what they practice? If they spent all their time practicing a good reaction to a touchdown, they would never score in a game. What do they do? They work on fundamentals.

In football practice, part of the time is spent developing the various muscles that will be used. The fellows also concentrate on the fundamentals of the game, like blocking and tackling. They work on plays and strategy. Later on, if they have mastered the fundamentals, they are going to score some touchdowns. But if they spend all of their time working on what to do in the thrilling moment, they will never have the chance to experience it in a game.

Most people make a similar mistake as they approach marriage. They say, "What's the thrilling part of marriage? Oh, it's the sensual, sexual part." And so a lot of people spend all their time working on that.

A recent list of the top ten best-sellers on college campuses included books on the techniques of sex. But students reading those books are working at the wrong end. If you do not have the phileo and agape love discussed earlier, all the techniques in the world will not give you a happy sex life.

Any marriage counselor dealing with people who are sexually impotent realizes that in practically every case, the cause is psychological and emotional rather than physical. An unsatisfactory sex life is generally brought about because they do not have agape and phileo love, or because of guilt.

If you really love and accept the other person; if you really enjoy being together and doing things together; if you are kind, considerate, patient, forgiving, and accepting, you will not have to worry about sex. It will come. You do not have to worry about how to show your excitement when you cross the goal line with the football; you will think of something. This is the way it is with sex. So spend your time working on the fundamentals.

You have three excellent training opportunities as you prepare to be marriageable: (1) your personal walk with Christ, (2) your home, and (3) your dating and other contacts with the opposite sex.

The first two are your best means for developing agape love, and the third can be used to develop your capacity for phileo love. We will examine each of these to see how to make the most of our opportunities.

YOUR PERSONAL WALK WITH CHRIST

How do you develop the capacity for true love? You cannot. It is humanly impossible. But you can experience true love. How? Read Galatians 5:22-23. Here we find that the qualities we need—love, joy, peace, longsuffering, gentleness, goodness, faith, meekness, and temperance—are the fruit of the Holy Spirit. The way to become a great lover, contrary to propaganda from Hollywood, is to cooperate with the Holy Spirit so He can produce His fruit in you.

Remember, it takes time to produce fruit. You don't plant apple seeds today and expect to pick apples tomorrow. If you postpone letting the Holy Spirit completely control your life until two or three years before marriage, you will not be ready. It takes more time.

The most important factor determining the kind of fruit produced is the seed sown. The Bible says you will reap what you sow. If you sow to the Spirit, you will reap a spiritual harvest; if you sow to the flesh, you will reap corruption (Galatians 6:7-8).

How do you sow? You plant ideas in your subconscious mind by reading, listening to the radio, or watching television or movies. In fact, everything you see, hear, touch, taste, or smell is recorded in the computer we call a brain. Check what you are taking in to see if you are sowing to the Spirit or the flesh. Do not

51

expect to be capable of Christian love if the bad seed outweighs the good.

The soil also is important. Jesus told a parable about four different types of soil, only one of which produced fruit. He compared the seed to the Word of God and the soil to those who receive the Word (Luke 8:4-15). The wayside represents those who turn off spiritual things completely. The rocky soil compares with people who have a surface, emotional experience only; their roots are not deep enough, and they fall when temptation comes. The thorny ground illustrates the response of those in whom the spiritual seed is choked by the cares and riches and pleasures of this life. The good soil speaks of the receptive spirit which, alone, produces fruit. What kind of soil are you?

In order to become marriageable we must give ardent attention to the seed we sow and to our reception of it.

YOUR HOME

As was mentioned in the last chapter, your home is one of your best training opportunities. It is at home that you must learn the sacrificial love necessary for a happy marriage.

Begin now to check your attitude at home. The following exercise should be helpful. First, go through and insert your name (the one you call yourself) in each blank. Then read it and see if it reads true.

1 Corinthians 13, taken from The Living Bible *with portions from the Phillips translation in parentheses:*

13:1. If _____ had the gift of being able to speak in other languages without learning them, and could speak in every language there is in all of heaven and earth, but didn't love others, _____ would be only making a noise.

13:2. If _____ had the gift of prophecy and knew all about what is going to happen in the future, knew everything about *everything*, but didn't love others, what good would it do? Even if _____ had the gift of faith so that _____ could speak to a mountain and make it move, _____ would still be worth nothing at all without love.

13:3. If _____ gave everything [he has] to poor people, and if _____ were burned alive for preaching the Gospel but didn't love others, it would be of no value whatever.

13:4. _____ is very patient and kind (slow to lose patience—[he] looks for a way of being constructive), never jealous or envious (is not possesive), never boastful or proud (is neither anxious to impress),

13:5. never haughty or selfish (nor does [he] cherish inflated ideas of [his] own importance) or rude (has good manners). _____ does not demand [his] own way (does not pursue selfish advantage). _____ is not irritable or touchy. _____ does not hold grudges and will hardly even notice when others do [him] wrong (does not keep account of evil).

13:6. _____ is never glad about injustice ([does not] gloat over the wickedness of other people), but rejoices whenever truth wins out.

13:7. If _____ love[s] someone, _____ will be loyal to him no matter what the cost (knows no limit to [his] endurance). _____ will always believe in him (no end to [his] trust), always expect the best of him (no fading of [his] hope), and always stand

53

[his] ground in defending him ([_____'s love]
can outlast anything. [His love] never fails.)

Now, go back to verse 4 and read through the exercise once for each member of your family, putting his
name at the end of each statement. For example, (your
name) is very patient with Daddy, kind to Daddy, et
cetera.

You may wish to concentrate on a different family
member each day. Use part of your quiet time to
examine your attitudes, decide on changes needed, and
pray for strength to correct particular areas.

If you cannot love under difficult circumstances at
home, you will not be able to after marriage. Learn to
live and love at home!

In addition to learning to love at home, make use of
every opportunity to learn homemaking skills. Helping
your parents with the chores is not only the loving
thing to do, but it trains you to do these things later.

YOUR DATING ACTIVITIES

What are some things you can do on a date that will
help you become marriageable and, at the same time,
help you choose the right person? We suggest these
four things: Work together, play together, think together, and worship together. You can have a great
time relating to the opposite sex in these ways. You get
to know people better by doing these things than in
any other way. Some people have gone steady for several years, dating three or four times a week, but after
marriage, they found out they were married to a total
stranger. You do not get to know anybody by smooch-
ing with him. You get to know him much better when
he hits his thumb with a hammer!

WORK TOGETHER

Shop together for the makings of pizza, fudge, or whatever you like to cook. Cook it together, eat it together, and clean up the mess together. Maybe some elderly couple in your neighborhood has to pay somebody to mow their lawn and cannot very well afford it. You and your date can have a wonderful time doing it for them. If she really enjoys riding around in that car of yours, maybe she would like to help wash and wax it some Saturday afternoon. Work at your church. Work really draws you together, and work for the Lord Jesus seems to do it even more.

PLAY TOGETHER

Perhaps you have gone steady with a certain person for a long time. Someone finally gets you two into a game of Monopoly, and suddenly it hits you how he thinks! "Hey, was I really going to marry that scoundrel?" you finally ask yourself in surprise.

You get to know people by playing. Play miniature golf, tennis, Ping-Pong, checkers, chess—anything you like to play. You get to know people as you play together.

THINK TOGETHER

Did you know that men and women are different in more than physical ways? If you do not know it, you better find it out before you get married! Talk about something that stretches your mind. Do you really get to know a person through conversation like the following?

"I love you."

"I love you, too."

"Your eyes are beautiful."

"Your eyes are beautiful, too."

"Your hair is nice."

"Your hair is OK."

Admittedly, a certain amount of that kind of talk is highly enjoyable. But let's face it—you don't get to know anybody that way! Talk about something that really makes you think. What should be done about poverty? How should Christians use their money? Discuss books you have read lately. Discuss priorities. Discuss viewpoints on various subjects. See how that fellow or girl thinks!

WORSHIP TOGETHER

Going to church is a great thing to do on a date, but worship is more than that. You ought to worship on every date. If you cannot pray on a date, there is something terribly wrong with you or the person you are dating.

You say, "How dull can you get?" But I say, "How romantic can you get?" There is nothing more wonderful than coming together at the end of an evening and thanking God for the wonderful time the *three* of you had together, because, you see, Jesus enjoyed that date, too. He doesn't get to go on many dates, because the Bible says that Jesus cannot look on sin. But the ones that He does get to go on, He enjoys, and He will help you enjoy them, too.

You say that's just too far out. But it happens. We have had it happen at our retreat center. In the summer we have college young people on our staff. One girl told me that one of the young staffers had invited her out on their day off. She said the first thing he did when they got in the car was to say, "Let's bow for a word of prayer before we go."

"I had the most wonderful time I have ever had on a date!" she told me with sparkling eyes. "You know, I never had a Christian date before, Mr. Rice. Oh, I've dated church members, but I never had a *Christian* date. There's a big difference! Believe me, I wouldn't think of going back to the other kind!"

Who ought to take the lead in the spiritual end of the date? Who is supposed to be the spiritual head of the home? The man. One of the biggest tricks the devil ever pulled on American society was to get us to think that it is manly to be naughty, that guys are supposed to be bad, and that girls are supposed to be sweet and hold the standards and say no.

Girls, if you have to say no, say no. But don't keep on dating him. And fellows, don't make her say no. You lead out in the spiritual end of the date. Don't think that a marriage ceremony will change you from the bad guy into the spiritual patriarch of the home. If you are not the spiritual leader on dates, you will not assume your place as the spiritual head of the home. Your home is not going to be what God meant it to be.

In order to develop properly our capability for phileo love, it is necessary to work, play, think, and worship with many different people of both sexes. Each adds something to your maturity. This is one reason that one of the most loving things you can do for the one you eventually marry is to go with a lot of different people before you settle on each other.

I know it is hard to be patient. We want the thrills now. We want the security of knowing whom we are going to marry. We fear that we may be left out or marry the wrong person.

In the next chapter, we will talk about choosing the right person. However, we must first be certain that we *become* the right person, so the one we choose will choose us. Do not consider wasted the years you spend becoming marriageable.

The Sermon on the Mount, found in Matthew 5-7, includes teachings on love, lust, marriage, divorce, and adultery. Jesus concluded this sermon with a parable about two builders. One built his house on a rock, and the other, on sand. Let's name the builders "Rocky" and "Sandy."

Sandy's house was going up while Rocky was still digging down. Sandy was enjoying his house while Rocky was still working on his foundation. When Rocky finally moved in, Sandy has been enjoying his house for days.

Which was the wise one? Jesus said the one who built on the rock. When the storms came, Rocky's house stood; Sandy's fell, and great was the fall of it.

Don't envy your friends who are already married, or who are experiencing sex outside marriage while you are still laying foundations. When the storms of life come—and they will—you will be very glad you were wise enough to put forth the effort necessary to become truly marriageable.

5

Choose Wisely

Besides becoming marriageable yourself, you will want to make sure that the person with whom you hope to spend your life is also marriageable. We have good news and bad news for you, as you think about choosing a mate.

The good news is that if you meet the biblical conditions for finding the will of God, and if you are supposed to marry, you *will* find the right person. God promises you will. You can prove what is the good and acceptable and perfect will of God (Romans 12:2). Proverbs 3:5-6 tells us that if we trust in the Lord with all our hearts and lean not on our own understanding, and if in all our ways we acknowledge Him, He *will* direct our paths. You can find the right person.

The bad news is that if you do not meet the conditions for finding the will of God, most likely you will end up with the wrong person. Many, many more people, even Christians, marry the wrong person than marry the right person. One reason for this is that most people pick the person they are going to marry for all the wrong reasons.

We will first discuss wrong ways to choose, then right ways, and end with a workable pattern.

WRONG WAYS TO CHOOSE

According to a certain authority on marriage, we choose a person in either affirmation or rejection of our parent of the opposite sex. That is, a girl who is really drawn to her father will pick some man who is like her dad or who in some way reminds her of him. A girl who is rebelling against her father might pick a man who is just the opposite of him. Fellows would be more influenced by their mothers.

Another reason that we choose certain persons is because of a subconscious reaction we have to them. I am sure you have met people to whom you were especially drawn when you first saw them. We call it love at first sight. Others you may dislike even though you do not really know them. Why? Perhaps something deep in your subconscious mind, that you could not possibly remember if you tried, triggered the positive or negative feelings.

For example, suppose that when you were two years old, someone gave you candy. Years later you meet someone else whose nose or hair or mouth subconsciously reminds you of the person who gave you the candy. You are drawn to him, you like him, and would love to spend time with him.

On the other hand, someone else reminds you of a person who stole your candy when you were two years old. You just cannot stand him and you do not know why. You are influenced by subconscious ideas which obviously have nothing to do with the person. He might not be at all like the person of whom you are subconsciously reminded, but your brain does not sort all that out. You just like him or dislike him for reasons that have nothing to do with the person himself.

Then again, you might make the same mistake that many people make—you might marry someone because he is a good date. But, you know, a person can be an ideal date and make a very sorry husband or wife!

The things that go into making a good date, generally speaking, have nothing to do with making a good husband or wife. In schools, the guys who are star athletes are at the top of the totem pole. They are the number one date bait. The girls who are cheerleaders or good dancers are very popular. But what does the ability to run with a football or yell or dance have to do with making a good husband or a good wife?

Good looks is a widely used, though very poor, criterion for selection. Research indicates that pretty girls are not, on the average, as happy in marriage as their plainer friends.

Unfortunately, even many Christians get their ideas about love and romance from television, music, movies, books, and magazines. In spite of the fact that most of these present a false view, they strongly influence our subconscious minds.

RIGHT WAYS TO CHOOSE

OK, so you agree that it is not smart to choose for the wrong reasons, and you want to choose for the right reasons. What do you do? We suggest the following steps.

CHOOSE BEFORE *EROS*

The first thing to do is to remember what we discussed in chapter 2 about being sure that the person is suitable for you before eros sets in, before you become blind. We compared choosing your socks before the lights go out to picking your mate before love blinds you. This does not mean that you necessarily would decide to marry the person. It means that before you become intimate with someone, you are sure the person would at least be suitable, on scriptural grounds, to be your husband or wife.

"Oh, I'm just going to date her," you say. "I'd never fall in love with her!" Well, that is one of those famous-last-words statements! Thousand of guys and girls have thought they would just date a few times— and then eros set in. They were blinded. They lost all ability to choose, and they ended up married to somebody completely unsuitable.

On television, you sometimes see a couple kiss and decide, as a result of the kiss, that they love each other. If you do not enjoy kissing your lover, there is something wrong; but the fact that you greatly enjoy kissing another person does not necessarily indicate real love. Kissing may prove enjoyable for many reasons, but it is certainly one of the poorest ways to choose a mate!

Perhaps some of you who read this have already come under the influence of eros, before developing the other kinds of relationships that we have talked about. How can you be sure? I would suggest a cooling-off period, a time in which you mutually agree to leave off physical intimacy to see if you can really enjoy each other in other ways.

A young Christian told me this was excellent advice but extremely difficult to follow. He said that he and his fiancée had agreed to call off all kissing and all other physical contact until marriage. They found no other way.

DECIDE ON LIFE PURPOSE

The next thing to do before you begin to settle in on one person is to decide on your life purpose. What is it? Is it to glorify God and bear fruit for Him and make disciples? Then everything else has to fit in with this number one priority.

With this in mind, ask yourself these questions: Should I continue my education? With what education can I best serve God? Where should I live? In what geographical location can I best serve God? What vocation should I choose? In what vocation can I bear the most fruit for God? Whom should I date? Whom should I marry? With what partner can I best serve God?

If Christ is number one, then all of our decisions must center around Him. That includes dating. The problem in teaching about Christian dating is that Christ is not number one in most people's lives. To most people, Christianity is just a side issue, something to take care of on Sunday. They do not want it to cramp their style or interfere with what they do the rest of the week. But remember, Christ must have first place.

KNOW WHAT YOU ARE LOOKING FOR

You are now ready to decide on the characteristics you would like in the person you marry. We often ask teenagers we counsel to list these qualities. A typical list is as follows: loving, patient, faithful, clean, good provider, good homemaker, dependable, good with children, neat, kind, sense of humor, loyal, unselfish, and trustworthy.

As we said previously, people are not naturally like that, but these qualities come from the Holy Spirit. Practically every characteristic people mention is covered by Paul's list of the fruit of the Spirit (Galatians 5:22-23), which includes love, joy, peace, patience, kindness, goodness, faithfulness, gentleness, and self-control.

Therefore, what we are really looking for is someone who is controlled by the Holy Spirit. When you are looking for somebody, do not ask how well he can dance or how well he can hit a tennis ball. Rather ask, To what extent is he controlled by the Holy Spirit of God?

Is that the way most of the young people in your school go about picking someone to date—the extent to which he or she is controlled by the Holy Spirit? Is that generally what they are looking for? And yet, when you think about it, this is what people really want.

Remember, a spiritual Christian is also looking for a person who is controlled by the Holy Spirit. The way to find that kind of person is to *be* that kind of person. It is only through the Holy Spirit that you can have a happy marriage. Only through Him can you continue to love people that inconvenience you and bear the other frustrations you will have in marriage. Remember that being the right kind of person is a lot harder than finding the right person!

You may wonder if you can ever find a person like that. It is true that there are not many around. The preacher of Ecclesiastes found only one man among a thousand and no women (Ecclesiastes 7:27-28). A woman doing the counting might have reached a different figure, but all can agree that the proportion of godly people is small indeed.

As we mentioned before, Jesus said the last days would be like the days of Noah, when only one family was right with God. Noah and his wife had three sons—the only three righteous boys in the whole world. And there were only three righteous girls in the world. What were the odds of their getting together? Practically nil. But they did. The three righteous boys found the three righteous girls. And so, if you *are* the right kind of person, you will find the right person.

I imagine those girls stayed home many lonely Saturday nights, don't you? I imagine Noah's sons missed many parties. But when the right time came, each found the right person. One in a thousand guys for one in a thousand girls is still one to one. And, after all, how many do you need?

Do not choose too soon

It is extremely important that you not attempt to choose your life's partner too soon. Statistics show that the best time to marry is between the ages of twenty-seven and thirty-one for men; for women the best age is twenty-five.[1] A recent *Reader's Digest* article said,

> Some marriages are programmed for early death at their birth—particularly among our youth. Americans become parents earlier than people in any other industrialized country. And the highest incidence of divorce is in the age group below 25—three times the overall rate. Wives under 20 are involved in more than half of all divorces yearly.[2]

Don't worry about choosing your life partner in high school. Chances are that, for a number of reasons, you will make the wrong choice. One reason is that in high school you do not yet know who you are. In fact, one of the leading questions asked on college campuses is, Who am I? So people are still trying to find out who they are in college. When you are young, you go through different stages. At one time you are in one stage and at another time in another stage. You could be in one stage in the tenth grade and in another stage in the twelfth grade, with yet more stages to come. If you fall in love with somebody in the tenth grade, each of you will be a different person when you are in the twelfth grade.

Another disadvantage of early marriage is that you have not had time to mature properly. The early years of marriage are critical and should not be entered into before you are ready. It would be a rare exception to find a man qualified to be a doctor by the age of twenty. Both statistics and common sense teach the same about marriage.

In high school and college, work on agape and phileo love. Develop the capacity to enjoy doing a lot of things with different people of the opposite sex.

"What if I've already found the right one?" you may ask. "If I go with other people, I may lose her!"

Listen, if you meet God's requirements, you will end up with the right person! That is a promise from God. So do not worry about losing her. Concentrate on developing yourself into the right kind of person.

I know it is hard sometimes not to want to hurry. I was twenty-six years old before I met the young lady I married when I was twenty-seven, and I thought God was dragging His feet. I was getting impatient and was trying to help Him out. I was looking all over the country for somebody to marry. When God's time arrived, He managed for me to meet, right in my small hometown of Belton, the girl I was supposed to marry.

It is a miracle the way He did it. He sent Vivian's brother-in-law to Belton to help open up a telephone office. Vivian came to visit her sister and brother-in-law, two blocks down the street from me. Her family and my family decided that we ought to meet, so they arranged for us to get together.

I had not known this wonderful girl existed. She lived over two hundred miles away from me. But when the right time came, when I was ready and she was ready, God brought us together. And God has kept us together, and we have had a beautiful, growing relationship.

Don't become impatient. Don't think you have to date every Tom or Sue that comes along. You may end up with the wrong mate. Do things God's way and become the kind of person that you want to marry, and you will end up with the right mate.

FOLLOW GOD'S KNOWN WILL NOW

Does this mean that we can wait until we are about ready to get married and then seek God's will? No! The way to find God's will *then* is to be in God's will *now*.

Take an example. A non-Christian guy asks a Christian girl to go steady. She knows it is not God's will because the Bible says to "be ... not unequally yoked ... with unbelievers" (2 Corinthians 6:14); but she does it anyway.

On their dates, he wants to take her to certain places, and she knows it is not God's will for her to go because the Bible says to "come out from among them and be ye separate" (2 Corinthians 6:17); but she goes anyway. When she gets there, he wants to do certain things, and she knows it is not God's will because the Bible says "keep thyself pure" (1 Timothy 5:22); but she does them anyway. Then she wonders why she cannot find God's guidance. Like most people, she marries the wrong person. Why? She was not following God's will when she knew it.

The Bible speaks of walking in the light (1 John 1:7). When that was written, they did not have powerful, far-reaching searchlights. They had tiny oil lamps that would probably light only about two or three steps.

"I've got to go a mile," you say. "I can't see my destination; I can't make it." The Bible says to walk in the light. So what do you do? You take a step, and you find your light moves a step, and you take another step and your light moves another step, always keeping just about a step ahead of you. But if you say, "Because I can't see my destination, I'll leave my light here and go off in darkness," you will be lost!

So the secret for finding God's will for tomorrow is to follow all the light we already have today. The Bible mentions three sources of light: Jesus (John 8:12), the Bible (Psalm 119:105), and other Christians (Matthew 5:14). If we follow all the light available from these sources, God will provide the needed light for tomorrow.

UNDERSTAND BIBLICAL MARRIAGE

God's plan and pattern for marriage has already been revealed in the Bible. As we briefly look at the requirements for a biblical marriage, consider if your love is sufficient. Carefully study this plan to see if you are willing to enter this type of relationship with the one you are thinking of marrying.

Wives are to submit to their husbands as unto the Lord (Ephesians 5:22); they are to be subject to their husbands in everything as the Church is to Christ (Ephesians 5:23); and they are to reverence their husbands (Ephesians 5:33). *The Living Bible* translates the first part of 1 Peter 3:1, "Wives, fit in with your husband's plans." Read Proverbs 31:10-31, a great passage on the godly wife.

Husbands are to love their wives as Christ loved the Church and gave Himself for it, "that He might sanctify and cleanse it ... that it should be holy and without blemish" (Ephesians 5:25-27). Fellows, do you have the kind of love that leads you to want to help your girl to become sanctified, pure, and holy, even though it involves great personal sacrifice?

Are you willing to be committed to this type of relationship for life, knowing that either of you could become an invalid? Are you certain enough of your love to be willing to make a public commitment?

If you are the man, are you sufficiently trained and prepared to assume your responsibilities as priest (spiritual leader), protector, and provider? If you are the woman, are you prepared to put being a homemaker high on your priority list? Are you both willing to sacrifice some of your ambitions for the success of the home?

OBTAIN PARENTAL ADVICE

One more thing to consider in choosing a mate is your parents' approval. Realizing that love would be blind, God has given us parents to help guide and advise us. Because of their years of experience, they can evaluate both you and your partner more objectively than you can. They may be able to see immaturity and problems of which you are totally unaware. Your parents may have some misgivings about anyone you go with. But if there are serious objections, you should listen.

Even non-Christians can be in God's chain of command (Romans 13:1-4). An authority does not have to be good, kind, or reasonable to command our respect (1 Peter 2:18). God can use evil men with completely selfish motives to accomplish His purpose (Genesis 50:20). Of course, our highest authority must always be God. If your parents try to persuade you to marry a non-Christian, you should refuse (Acts 5:29).

A WORKABLE PATTERN

Let's look now at a pattern that can lead to real, lasting love.

Begin now to develop agape love at home, at school, and in all your associations. Practice doing the loving thing regardless of your feelings.

At the same time, begin to cultivate friendships with both sexes, which will increase your capability for phileo love. There is a very encouraging trend toward this on college campuses, where Spirit-controlled students meet together in fellowship, Bible study, and prayer groups. Rather than just dating one at a time, they do a lot of things in groups. They work together, play together, think together, and worship together, as was suggested in the last chapter. This helps develop their capacity for agape and phileo love.

As you work, play, think, and worship with the opposite sex, there will come times when two of you are especially happy doing things together. You have many common interests. You enjoy discussing things of importance. You feel comfortable in each other's presence. You can be completely honest. In times of special joy or sorrow, it is good to have this person with whom to share.

While you do not neglect your other friends, there

will be times when the two of you want to go out alone. You enjoy being together, just the two of you.

Over a period of time, there will probably be several different persons with whom you have this type of relationship. You learn and grow in each experience.

You will not be under the pressure of fearing that you might lose the one you are meant to marry. You have faith that, as a result of following the principles previously given, you will end up with the right person.

A time will come when one relationship stands out from all the others. Since you have had meaningful relationships with a number of different people, you have an excellent basis for comparison. You are not in danger of being fooled by eros, because it has played a very minor part up to this point.

If you have peace about all this as you pray, you are ready to commit yourselves to each other publicly and legally as well as before God. Why not just to God? Well, adultery is not just having sex with someone you do not love; it is having sex with anyone to whom you are not legally married. One of the essentials of marriage in our society is that it be on public record.

You will begin marriage with the satisfaction of knowing everything is proper and under the lordship of Christ. You will be glad you followed Him instead of yielding to your feelings or to the crowd.

We received a card from a girl who had heard us teach some of these principles. Would you believe she wrote us on her honeymoon to thank us? The discussions had helped her to do things God's way, and she was so grateful that she just had to let us know.

Another girl stopped by to spend a weekend with us. Though only in her early twenties, she was already separated from her husband. "You don't know how often I've thought about the talks on dating I heard you give," she told us. "How I wish I had followed the advice!"

6

But What If–? What About–?

These are questions that teenagers have asked us.

What if a boy won't date you if you don't make out?

Give him up. You really have not lost anything. The type of life we are recommending is not for everyone. Only a few are on the narrow road that leads to life (Matthew 7:13), but they do find what the others are really looking for.

If this happens to you often, you should check on what you are advertising. For example, suppose I am trying to sell lemonade. I have a beautiful lemonade stand, but I do not have a sign. So I go down to the junk yard and find a well-made sign that says "Ice Cold Beer," and I put the beer sign up in front of my lemonade stand. You see a lot of traffic stopping and ask, "How's business?"

"I haven't sold a single glass of lemonade."

"Well, I saw a lot of cars stop."

"Yes, a lot of people stopped, but everybody that stopped wanted beer. I can't understand it. Nobody who stops wants lemonade."

Why? Because I am *advertising* beer.

Suppose a girl advertises, by the way she dresses and acts, that her body is available cheap. Who is going to answer the ad? You know who—the guys who want a body that is available cheap. If you do not give them what they want, are they going to come back? No.

Suppose a guy advertises by the way he dresses—and this varies from school to school and time to time—that he is a rebel. Who is going to want to date him?

If you go out with certain types, people will say you are that sort of person. That will limit the people you date, won't it?

How can I find Christians to date?

One way to find the right person is to go where Christians hang out. We had a friend who was very upset because her daughter could not seem to find any Christian gentlemen to date. We told her about several places where Christian young people would be gathering. But the girl did not want to go to any Christian retreats or conferences. She wanted to go only to dances and parties. Then she wondered why she could not find a Christian to marry!

If you want a fine Christian person, go where Christians hang out. It is important to discover where the real Christian action is and not just churchianity.

What about dating non-Christians?

The Bible specifically warns against this in 2 Corinthians 6:14-17. The command is, "Be not unequally yoked together with unbelievers." A yoke was a wooden frame joining two oxen. As Paul uses the term, it would seem to imply a binding or obligating relationship as opposed to a casual friendship. The command is followed with an explanation. Christ, on the throne in a Christian's heart, cannot have fellowship with Satan, who is on the throne in every non-Christian's life. The only way to have real fellowship with a non-Christian would be to take Christ off the throne of your life.

Many other Scriptures warn us against the wrong kind of friendship with non-Christians. Among these are Psalm 1:1; Ephesians 5:11; 1 Corinthians 5:9-13; 2 Thessalonians 3:6; 2 Timothy 3:5; 2 John 10-11. The references in 1 Corinthians, 2 Thessalonians, and 2 Timothy deal with those who call themselves Christians but who do not live the Christian life.

While we cannot say that the Bible positively forbids dating non-Christians, many young people have found this to be the most practical solution. Knowing when and how to end relationships with non-Christians without hurting their feelings seems harder than having a policy of not dating them at all. The advantages of a fixed policy will be discussed further under the question, "But what if you don't know if he's a Christian?"

But what if I want to witness to them?

Of course we are to witness to non-Christians. But you do not need to run the risk of getting emotionally involved with non-Christians of the opposite sex in order to witness to them.

Girls, if you are truly burdened for lost young

people, invite a half-dozen or a dozen girls to your home for a pajama party. Get out your Bible and share what Christ means to you, and tell them how they can know Him, too. Guys, plan an overnight or an all-day hike with fellows you want to witness to. Share the Gospel with them when you sit around the campfire.

Are you really doing all the witnessing you could be doing in non-dating situations? If you are, it is doubtful that you will feel the need to *date* a non-Christian in order to witness.

Not only is dating non-Christians dangerous, but it is not really the best way to reach people. Any soul-winner will tell you that it is easier to reach people with whom you are not emotionally involved than those with whom you are emotionally involved. If your real motive is to witness to a person, the last thing to do is date him. Several great soul-winners have asked us to witness to members of their families because they were "too close" to them. Even Jesus did not reach His own brothers. They thought He was a fool until after the resurrection, after He had physically left the scene. Do not date a person in order to witness to him.

If your relationship proceeds to the point that you are yoked to the unbeliever, you cannot even pray for the person. The Bible says that "God heareth not sinners: but if any man be a worshipper of God, and doeth his will, him he heareth" (John 9:31). I cannot pray for someone else if I am not in the will of God myself, and it is not in the will of God for me to be in that kind of relationship.

Furthermore, witnessing is not a good excuse for obligating involvement with non-Christians. Would it be OK for me to rob a bank if I witnessed to the bank teller while I was robbing it? You know the answer to that easily enough! Violating any command of God for the excuse of witnessing is wrong.

Another reason for not pairing off with unbelievers is that you are much more likely to be pulled down than the other person is to be pulled up. Imagine you are standing on a table and grasping the hand of someone on the floor. Is it easier for you to pull him up or for him to pull you down? It is always easier to be pulled down. Consequently, to serve God and prepare for marriage, do not become intimate with people who are not Spirit filled.

But what about Jesus fellowshipping with sinners?

Two passages in the Bible are used most often to prove that we should associate with sinners. And to a certain extent, we should be involved with sinners. But we must be certain that we are following the biblical pattern regarding the nature of the association.

The first passage is about Jesus and the adulterous woman at the well in Samaria (John 4:4-43). There are three reasons why Jesus might not have spoken to this woman. First, she was a woman, and men did not speak to strange women. Second, she was a Samaritan, and Jews did not speak to Samaritans. Third, she was a sinner.

The Samaritan woman mentions two of those reasons in verse 9. She asked Jesus, "How is it that thou, being a Jew, asketh drink of me, which am a woman of Samaria?"

What did He do? He spoke to her anyway.

Is that an excuse for dating and running around with the wrong crowd? How long did Jesus dillydally around before He got God into the picture? The very second thing He said was that God wanted to give her what she was really looking for. Jesus was saying that God was the answer to her real need.

The woman was obviously impressed. But Jesus did not tell her to bow down and receive Christ; He told her to go get her husband (v. 16). Why did He tell her that? It was to point out her besetting sin. Jesus had to get her sin into the picture. "The woman answered and said, I have no husband. Jesus said unto her, Thou hast well said, I have no husband: for thou hast had five husbands; and he whom thou now hast is not thy husband: in that saidst thou truly" (v. 17-18).

You have heard of the new morality—of people living together who are not married. Is there anything new about that way of living? No. That is what the Samaritan woman was doing.

After further conversation, in which she tried to get Jesus off the subject, she finally believed that He was the Messiah. It hit her so hard that she dropped her water jar and hastened to the town to tell the people!

Did Jesus escort her back to town? Obviously, she was planning to come back, because she left her water jar at the well. Wouldn't escorting her home be the gentlemanly thing to do? Why didn't He do it?

Suppose He had escorted her and had gone into her home. Do you think the great revival would have taken place? Verse 39 reports that many people believed on Jesus because of the testimony of the woman. If He had spent time in her home, do you think all those men would have come out?

"Yeah, I've been in that house, too," some might have said. "I don't blame him for going there. I had a pretty good time there myself."

No, Jesus did His talking in the most public place in

town—the well—where there could not be a hint of scandal. He immediately brought God into the picture. The way some people seem to interpret the story is that Jesus was concerned for this woman, so He started dating her. After a long time of becoming intimate, He casually dropped a hint about coming to church sometime. That's not the way He did it, is it?

Be sure that, if you are going to use that passage, you act the way Jesus did. He did not even escort the woman home. No one could think that He was part of what she stood for, as they might have thought had He gone.

Luke 5 is used perhaps even more frequently to justify the wrong kind of relationship with non-Christians. In Luke 5:30, the Pharisees and scribes accused Jesus of eating and drinking with sinners. Did He deny this? No, verse 31 says that is what He came for. But verse 32 tells what He was doing with sinners when He was with them. He was calling them to repent. Don't ever use this as an excuse for running around with the wrong crowd unless you do what Jesus did: unless you call them to repent.

Who was the particular sinner Jesus was accused of eating with, anyway? It was Levi, better known as Matthew. What had Matthew just done in verse 28? He had forsaken everything to follow Jesus. Many who use this as an excuse for fellowshipping with sinners have never backed up to see who the particular sinner was and what that sinner had just done. The sinner had just forsaken everything to follow Jesus.

How do you break off with the wrong crowd?

Do what Matthew did. Throw a party. He invited all

his old sinner friends. Matthew knew what a lot of people today do not. Many have the idea, "Well, I'll try to let people gradually see a change in me, and I'll try to ease away from the bad crowd and ease into the good crowd." That will not work.

If you run around with the wrong crowd, if you are dating a non-Christian, do what Matthew did and have a party. Invite all your sinner friends to the party. The Bible says a great company came. Why did so many people come to Matthew's party? Perhaps they had been to parties at Matthew's house before and had a ball. But this party was different. Jesus was there.

We are not told exactly what Matthew said, but I think we can guess pretty well. He must have said something like this, "Friends, you know you are my friends and that I love you. We've had some great times together, and I really value your friendship, but I had an experience that changed my whole life. I met Jesus Christ personally! I'm giving up my job. I'm changing my life-style. And from this point on, I'm going to be a different person. I hope every one of you will join me, but whether you do or not, I'm going to follow Him." And then he introduced them to Jesus, the One who had made it possible.

You see how much better that is? Suppose you have friends whom you have told about lying to your parents, or with whom you have exchanged dirty jokes. Do not say, "I'm just gradually going to be a little bit different and let them see."

Instead, call them all together and say, "I had an experience that led me to change my life. I know it's going to be hard, and I have a lot of growing to do. I know I've sinned with you, and I know you've heard and seen me do unchristian things, and I'm sorry. From this point on I'm going to try my best to be different. I hope you'll be different with me, but whether you are or not, I'm going to follow Jesus."

Do it that way, and you have a great chance of making it. Try to break away gradually, and your friends will probably pull you down instead of you pulling them up.

But what if you can't give them up?

A girl once told me that she could not give up her boyfriend, even though he was not a Christian. "You just can't give up someone you love," she said.

Well, if you cannot give someone up, you cannot be a Christian! Luke 14:26 says, "If any man come to me, and hate not his father, and mother, and wife, and children, and brethren, and sisters, yea, and his own life also, he cannot be my disciple." We might add boyfriend or girl friend to the list. "Hate," in this passage, is generally interpreted as illustrating how little love we should have for these people in comparison to our love for God.

One consolation is that we are promised at any loss we suffer for Christ will be made up to us at least one-hundred times (Mark 10:29-30). Does this mean God will give you one-hundred boyfriends or girl friends? Perhaps. But more likely, He will give you *one* a hundred times better than a non-Christian steady.

But what if you don't know if he's a Christian?

First, if he is someone you know well and you do not know if he is a Christian, then he isn't one. At least he is not the kind of Christian we are talking about. A true Christian will be vocal about his faith.

But there are occasions when you do not know a person that well. Perhaps you are a Christian girl who has classes with a guy or sees him on occasions where there is no real opportunity for conversation. If he asks you out, your reply might be something like this:

SHE: "I really do appreciate your asking me and would like to go out with you. But I once made a commitment not to date people who don't feel about Jesus the way I do."

HE: "How do you know how I feel?"

SHE: "I don't, but I would like to. Would you like to come to my house Friday evening so we can share our views with each other?"

If he comes, isn't that a date? Yes, but it is a date on the Christian's terms. It is for the specific purpose of discussing Christ. That makes it like Matthew's party, mentioned earlier. The sinners were at the party, but on the Christian's terms. Of course, you may prefer to meet him after school, during lunch, or at some other convenient time. But meet him at a safe place.

Before you can use this approach, you must have made a definite commitment not to date unbelievers. If you have not, why not do so right now so you will be ready when the occasion arises? Your previous commitment saves hurting the other's feelings, since your reply is not due to any failure on his part.

How do you think a guy would respond? Most would probably tell you to forget it. You have lost a date, but what have you really lost? Nothing. Dedicated Christian young men, however, would jump at an opportunity like that. We know many young men who have said they would be thrilled by such a girl.

What about going steady?

First, let's look at some of the advantages. You do not have to worry about getting dates for events. It is nice to have somebody you can call your own. You can get to know the person well and can relax with him. Many feel that they are really in love with that particular person and wouldn't want to go with anyone else.

Now, consider the disadvantages. A number have been mentioned in previous chapters, and you may wish to read those portions again. In chapter 3, we discussed the law of diminishing returns as it affected physical intimacy. The tendency to progress a little further on each date is extremely dangerous.

Also, reread the section "Love is never jealous or envious" in chapter 2. The following points were made, which you need to keep in mind as you decide what to do:
1. Real love puts the happiness of the other first.
2. Don't be afraid of losing your steady if he goes with others. If he would be happier with someone else, then the sooner you find it out, the better.
3. You can each become more mature by going with others.
4. You are more likely to know the right one if you have a broad basis for comparison.
5. Going steady limits associations with your own sex as well as with the opposite sex. And it often results in marrying too soon. The danger of this was discussed in chapter 5.

What about kissing on early dates?

What does a kiss mean to you? Some girls reply that it is just a way of saying thank you. Why not just say thank you, and save your kisses until they can mean more? If you kiss on early dates, what are you going to do later, when you have really established a special relationship?

Some fear that if they do not kiss, their date will feel rejected. Of course, if you have a reputation for kissing anyone you go out with, a person you do not kiss would have a right to be hurt. For example, a girl who usually kisses her dates the first night would insult a boy she refused to kiss until the fifth date. On the other hand, a girl who ordinarily does not kiss until the twentieth date would flatter a guy she kissed on the tenth.

A better way is to work, from the very beginning, on the type of relationship described in this book, agape and phileo love. How do you get started on this basis? One way would be to give him or her a copy of this book and agree to discuss it on future dates.

But what if you really like him and want to let him know?

We once took a poll among teens. Practically all agreed that the fellow should come right out and tell the girl he likes her. A few thought the girl could state her feelings, but the overwhelming majority felt that she should not do so first.

There are other ways, however, of letting him know. A special smile and squeeze of the hand from some girls says "You are special" much more clearly than heavy necking and petting do.

A girl received a letter from a boy saying, "You are the only girl in all the world for me." She was thrilled until she noticed the letter was mimeographed. If your favors are mass produced, they don't mean anything.

Often a girl gives in to a fellow and then finds that he does not love her anymore. This may be because of the inborn desire for the forbidden fruit, a desire we inherited from Adam. After the conquest is over, he loses interest.

The Bible describes such an incident, in which Amnon wanted Tamar so much he became ill. After he lay with her, he "hated her with a very great hatred; for the hatred with which he hated her was greater than the love with which he had loved her. And Amnon said to her, 'Get up, go away!' " (2 Samuel 13:15, NASB).

What about infatuation and crushes?

Infatuation and crushes generally center on highly visible surface characteristics rather than on intimate knowledge of the inner person. We may have many reasons for feeling romantically inclined toward certain persons. We may have feelings toward a television star, sports hero, older person, or other idol where no real relationship is practical. We may also have these feelings toward someone who is eligible, with whom we could develop a meaningful relationship. The point is that we should not trust these feelings until we have a strong agape and phileo relationship with the person.

If we commit ourselves to each other in private, is a marriage ceremony necessary?

Since marriage customs vary, many young people may ask, "Why is a ceremony necessary at all? If you commit yourselves to each other, isn't that enough?"

The Bible teaches that adulterers and fornicators will

85

not inherit the Kingdom of God (1 Corinthians 6:9-10). Adultery is voluntary sexual intercourse between a married person and anyone other than the lawful spouse. Fornication is voluntary sexual intercourse on the part of an unmarried person with a person of the opposite sex. Both fornicators and adulterers are included in the list of those who will not inherit the Kingdom of God.

What are the requirements for marriage in the sight of God? Though customs and laws vary, the following items are always necessary.

1. Permanence. If you are married in the sight of God, you should not be able to walk away from the relationship (Mark 10:9). Divorces were permitted in certain cases, but a written bill was necessary (Mark 10:4). Jesus said, however, that provision for divorce was made only because of the hardness of men's hearts (Mark 10:5) and was not God's plan.

Some young people today have changed the marriage vows from "as long as we both shall live" to "as long as we both shall love." Though legal, this is not Christian marriage. Christian marriage must be for life.

2. Public commitment. Marriage is not just a private affair, as many assume. It affects entire societies. You must be either married or not married in the eyes of society; there can be no middle ground.

3. Legal rights and obligations. Marriage must bind both parties legally (Romans 7:2; 1 Corinthians 7:39). Each party has certain rights which can be enforced by law if the other fails to fulfill certain obligations. In the event of death, there are very important legal considerations, such as social security benefits, inheritance rights, and responsibility for any children, which must be faced.

Some think that the idea of living together without a valid marriage is modern. This is ridiculous. The fourth chapter of John describes the encounter between Jesus and a woman who was living with a man to whom she was not legally married. Did the fact that they loved each other enough and were committed to each other enough to live together make them married? No! Jesus said the man with whom she was living was not her husband (John 4:18).

What about sex during engagement?

Sexual intercourse during engagement is fornication, and no fornicators will inherit the Kingdom of God (1 Corinthians 6:9-10). The desire to avoid the terrible consequences of fornication should be reason enough to abstain from it, but there are several other good reasons.

Engagements are often broken. I know you think this could not happen in your case, but it has happened to others who thought the same thing. Of course, there is always the chance of death.

Another strong reason for waiting is that otherwise the partners would always know that their sex life had not been under the control of God. They would always have a sense of guilt, and they could never have the complete freedom that comes from knowing that they did things God's way.

How can you resist the strong pressure to go too far with someone you love enough to marry? Do not allow yourself to get into tempting situations. Plan activities that are safe. Work, play, think, and worship together. Watch for danger signals.

What if you have already gone too far?

We have referred several times to 1 Corinthians 6:9-10, stating that adulterers and fornicators will not inherit the Kingdom of God. The very next verse, however, says: "And such were some of you: but ye are washed, but ye are sanctified, but ye are justified in the name of the Lord Jesus, and by the Spirit of our God."

Note the three things this verse says the Spirit of God wants to do for you.

First, you are *washed*. When He washes you, you become clean and pure. You do not have to feel dirty anymore.

Second, you are *sanctified*. This means you become holy, hallowed, set apart for God.

Third, you are *justified*. This means you are made righteous in the sight of God. The Law is satisfied.

Isn't that a wonderful package? Paul also tells us, "Therefore if any man be in Christ, he is a new creature: old things are passed away; behold, all things are become new" (2 Corinthians 5:17).

Right now, you can be born again. You can become a new creature. You can be clean and pure and holy. How? By receiving Jesus as your Saviour and Lord. You may think you already did that before you sinned. Numerous passages, including 1 Corinthians 6:9-10, Galatians 5:19-21, and 1 John 2:4, indicate that if you have been committing adultery or fornication since then, you may not have been truly saved at that time. Your actions should at least lead you to follow Paul's admonition, "Test yourselves to see if you are in the faith; examine yourselves!" (2 Corinthians 13:5*a*, NASB).

You may have had all kinds of religious experiences

and have really thought you were saved. But so did the people in Matthew 7:21-23. They had faith enough to call Jesus "Lord," to prophesy in His name, and to perform great works in His name. They "just knew" they were saved, but they weren't. They did not have faith enough to do the will of God.

But don't all Christians sin? Yes. But the Bible distinguishes between willful sins and sins which are not deliberate (Hebrews 10:26). Our laws today do the same. There is a big difference between premeditated murder and other types of homicide. Fornication and adultery are willful, premeditated sins. You have to make arrangements. You have to have a place. You have to take off at least part of your clothes. There are lots of chances to stop short of sexual intercourse if you really want to.

In Romans 7:14-25, Paul describes his continuing sinful nature. He failed to do the good he wanted to do and continued to do the evil things he hated. But his *desire* was to obey God—the *will* was present. This is quite different from one who *wills* to continue to live a life in rebellion against the known will of God.

I am not saying that there has never been a Christian who has committed adultery or fornication. I am saying that if you have committed these sins, then you have reason to doubt. What do you do if you have doubts? Let me tell you what I did.

I have never commited the particular sins referred to above. But when I found out what saving faith really was, I did have a little doubt. And a little doubt is too much with eternity, heaven, and hell, at stake. So I prayed a prayer like this:

"God, you know I think I'm a Christian, but I'm not 100 percent positive. So right now I want to make sure.

If I am saved, give me the assurance of it. If I am not saved, save me right now, because I am trusting you as Saviour—the One who provided for my salvation on the cross—and as Lord—the One I will obey."

If you are not certain you are saved, will you make certain right now? Begin to experience the abundant life Christ came to give! Then you can have His guidance and the power of the Holy Spirit working in your life to make it possible for you to experience true love in a lasting marriage.

Notes

CHAPTER 2

1. Henry A. Overstreet, *The Mature Mind* (New York: Norton, 1969), p. 103.

CHAPTER 5

1. Marcia E. Lasswell, "Is There a Best Age to Marry?: An Interpretation," *The Family Coordinator*, July 1974, p. 240.
2. Lester Velie, "What's Killing Our Marriage?" *Reader's Digest*, June 1973, pp. 152-156.